In Honor Of
MW01622070

Thoughts & Memories

Name:

Name:

Name:

In a moment, everything can change.

Firefighters know this *better than all.*

Thoughts & Memories

Name:

Name:

Name:

Yet they're willing to serve.

Always on-call.

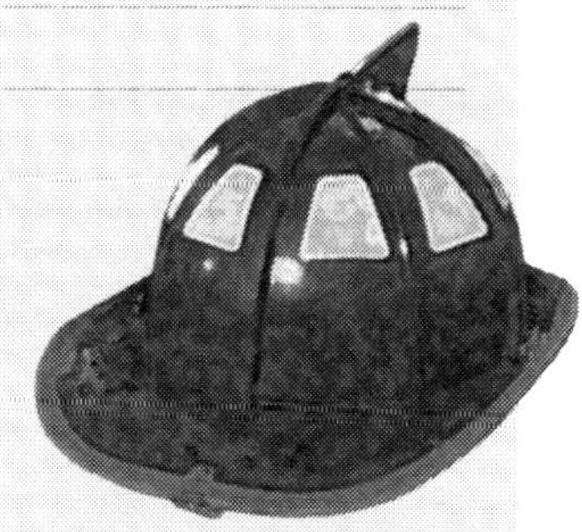

Thoughts & Memories

Name:

Name:

Name:

In a moment, everything can change.

Firefighters know this *better than all.*

Thoughts & Memories

Name:

Name:

Name:

Yet they're willing to serve.

Always on-call.

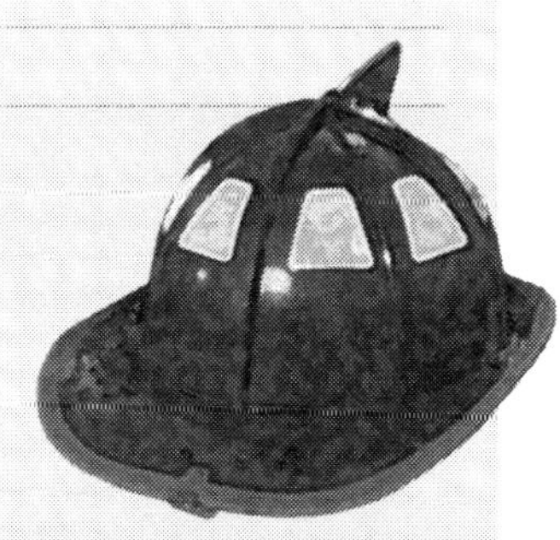

Thoughts & Memories

Name:

Name:

Name:

In a moment, everything can change.

Firefighters know this *better than all.*

Thoughts & Memories

Name:

Name:

Name:

Yet they're willing to serve.

Always on-call.

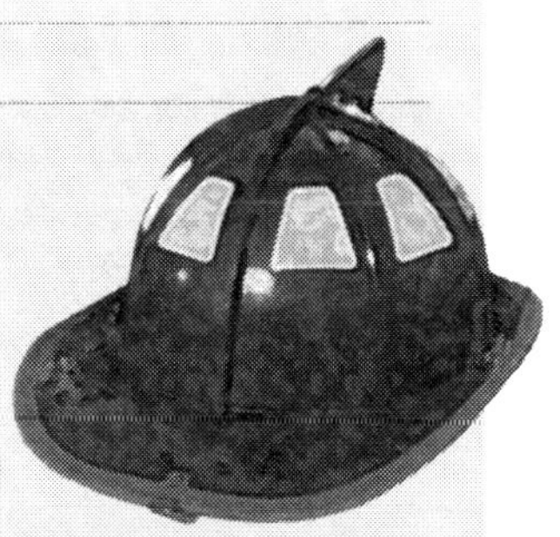

Thoughts & Memories

Name:

Name:

Name:

In a moment, everything can change.

Firefighters know this *better than all.*

Name:

Name:

Name:

Thoughts & Memories

Yet they're willing to serve.

Always on-call.

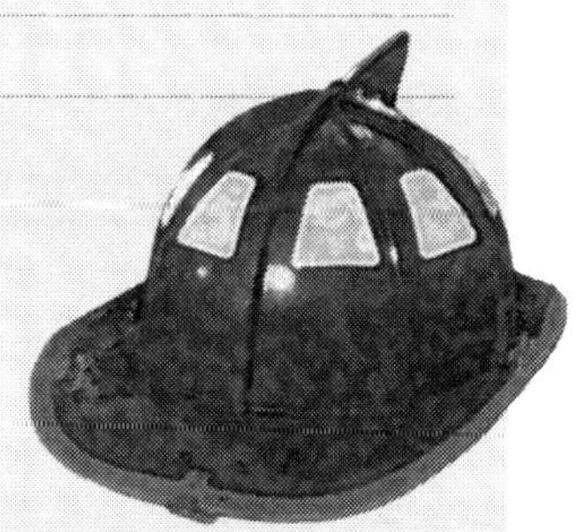

Thoughts & Memories

Name:

Name:

Name:

In a moment, everything can change.

Firefighters know this *better than all.*

Name:

Name:

Name:

Thoughts & Memories

Yet they're willing to serve.

Always on-call.

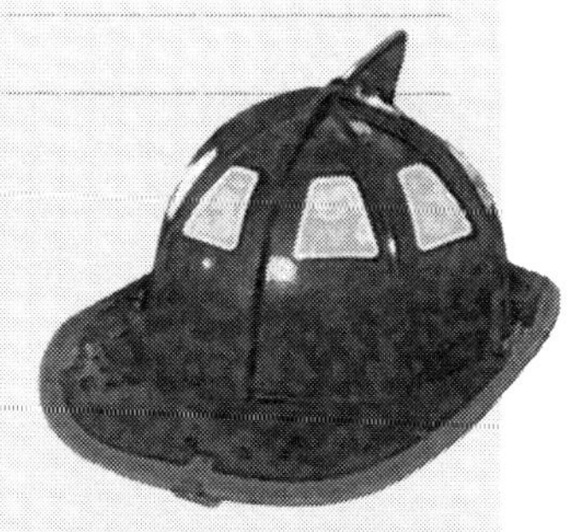

Thoughts & Memories

Name:

Name:

Name:

In a moment, everything can change.

Firefighters know this *better than all.*

Thoughts & Memories

Name:

Name:

Name:

Yet they're willing to serve.

Always on-call.

Thoughts & Memories

Name:

Name:

Name:

In a moment, everything can change.

Firefighters know this *better than all.*

Name:

Name:

Name:

Thoughts & Memories

Yet they're willing to serve.

Always on-call.

Thoughts & Memories

Name:

Name:

Name:

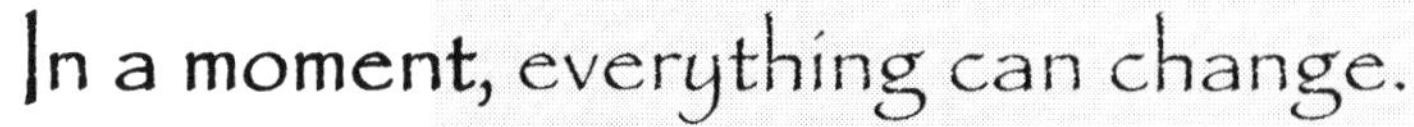

In a moment, everything can change.

Firefighters know this *better than all.*

Name:

Name:

Name:

Thoughts & Memories

Yet they're willing to serve.

Always on-call.

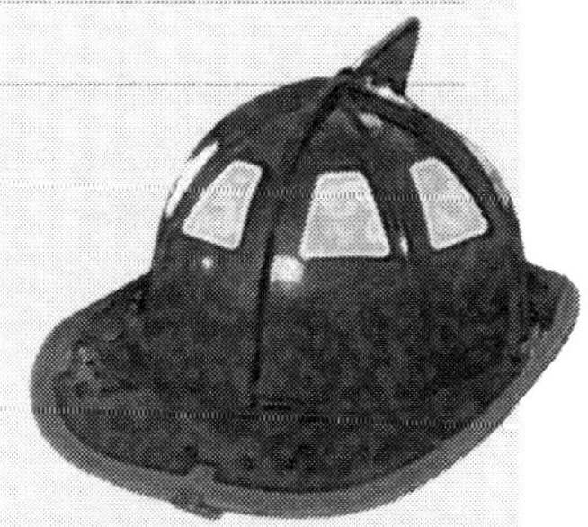

Thoughts & Memories

Name:

Name:

Name:

In a moment, everything can change.

Firefighters know this *better than all.*

Name:

Thoughts & Memories

Name:

Name:

Yet they're willing to serve.

Always on-call.

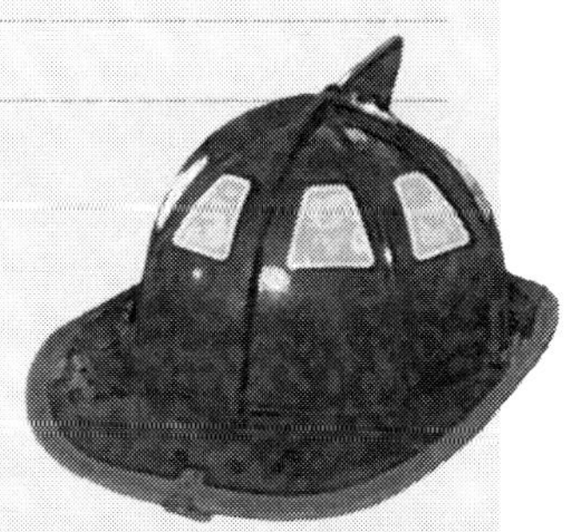

Thoughts & Memories

Name:

Name:

Name:

In a moment, everything can change.

Firefighters know this *better than all.*

Name:

Name:

Name:

Thoughts & Memories

Yet they're willing to serve.

Always on-call.

Thoughts & Memories

Name:

Name:

Name:

In a moment, everything can change.

Firefighters know this *better than all.*

Thoughts & Memories

Name: ______________________

Name: ______________________

Name: ______________________

Yet they're willing to serve.

Always on-call.

Thoughts & Memories

Name:

Name:

Name:

In a moment, everything can change.

Firefighters know this *better than all.*

Name:

Name:

Name:

Thoughts & Memories

Yet they're willing to serve.

Always on-call.

Thoughts & Memories

Name:

Name:

Name:

In a moment, everything can change.

Firefighters know this *better than all.*

Thoughts & Memories

Name:

Name:

Name:

Yet they're willing to serve.

Always on-call.

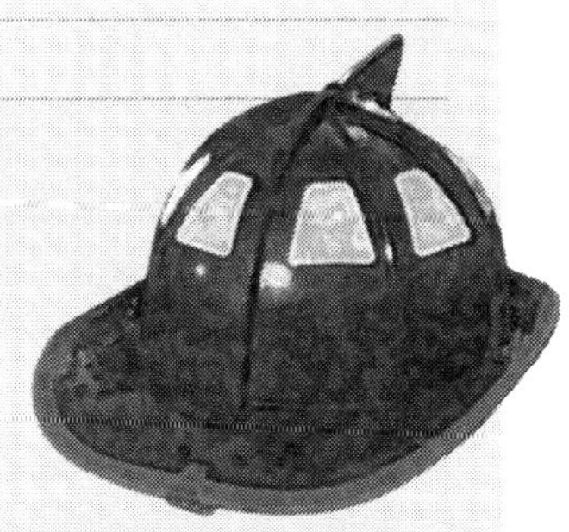

Thoughts & Memories

Name:

Name:

Name:

In a moment, everything can change.

Firefighters know this *better than all.*

Name:

Name:

Name:

Thoughts & Memories

Yet they're willing to serve.

Always on-call.

Thoughts & Memories

Name:

Name:

Name:

In a moment, everything can change.

Firefighters know this *better than all.*

Thoughts & Memories

Name:

Name:

Name:

Yet they're willing to serve.

Always on-call.

Thoughts & Memories

Name:

Name:

Name:

In a moment, everything can change.

Firefighters know this *better than all.*

Thoughts & Memories

Name:

Name:

Name:

Yet they're willing to serve.

Always on-call.

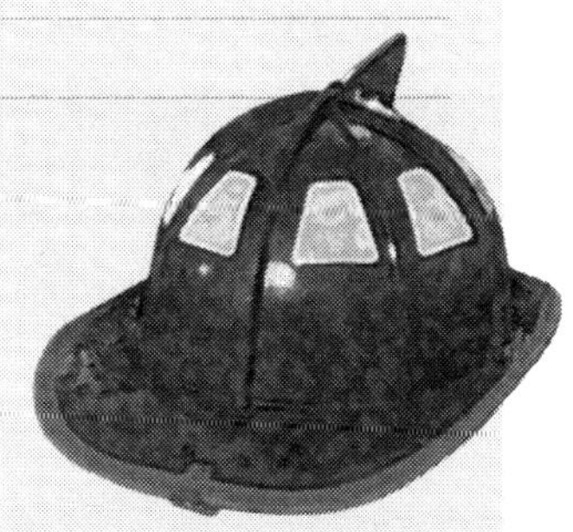

Thoughts & Memories

Name:

Name:

Name:

In a moment, everything can change.

Firefighters know this *better than all.*

Thoughts & Memories

Name: ______________________

Name: ______________________

Name: ______________________

Yet they're willing to serve.

Always on-call.

Thoughts & Memories

Name:

Name:

Name:

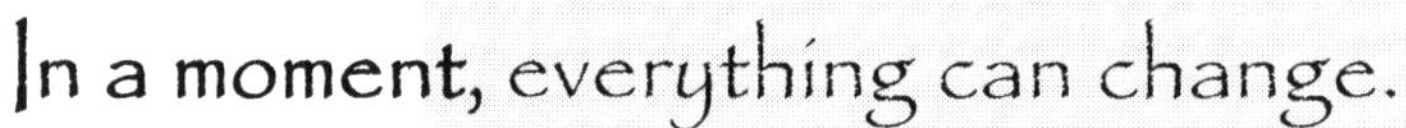

In a moment, everything can change.

Firefighters know this *better than all.*

Name:

Name:

Name:

Thoughts & Memories

Yet they're willing to serve.

Always on-call.

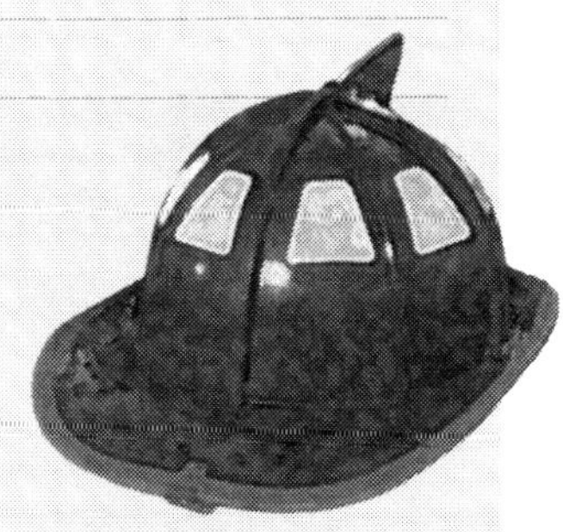

Thoughts & Memories

Name:

Name:

Name:

In a moment, everything can change.

Firefighters know this *better than all.*

Name:

Name:

Name:

Thoughts & Memories

Yet they're willing to serve.

Always on-call.

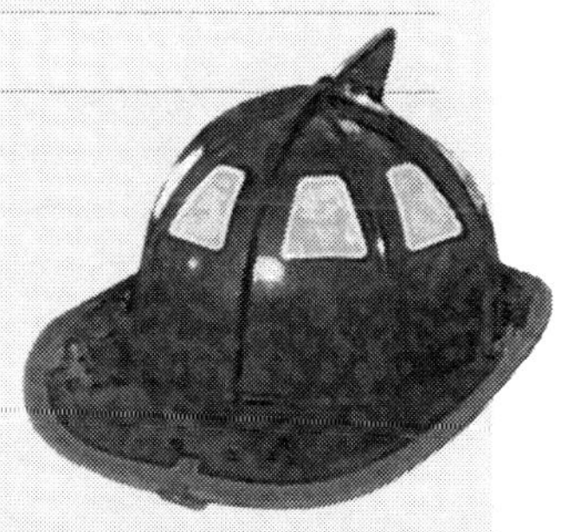

Name:

Thoughts & Memories

Name:

Name:

In a moment, everything can change.

Firefighters know this *better than all.*

Thoughts & Memories

Name:

Name:

Name:

Yet they're willing to serve.

Always on-call.

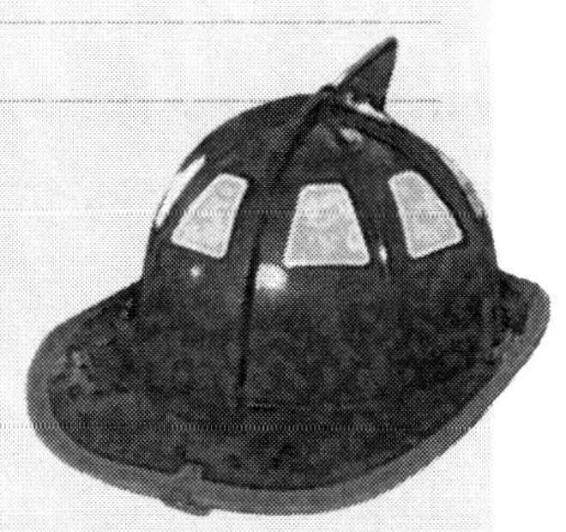

Name:

Name:

Name:

Thoughts & Memories

In a moment, everything can change.

Firefighters know this *better than all.*

Name:

Name:

Name:

Thoughts & Memories

Yet they're willing to serve..

Always on-call.

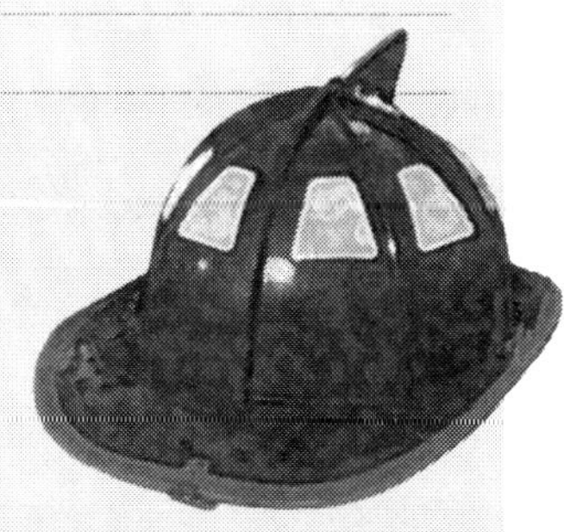

Thoughts & Memories

Name:

Name:

Name:

In a moment, everything can change.

Firefighters know this *better than all.*

Name:

Name:

Name:

Thoughts & Memories

Yet they're willing to serve.

Always on-call.

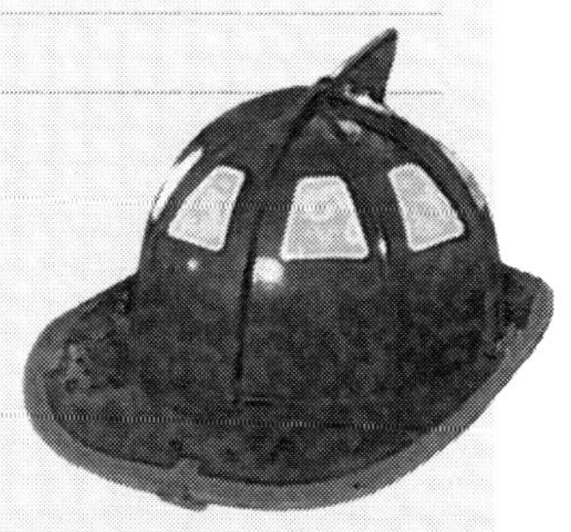

Thoughts & Memories

Name:

Name:

Name:

In a moment, everything can change.

Firefighters know this *better than all.*

Thoughts & Memories

Name:

Name:

Name:

Yet they're willing to serve.

Always on-call.

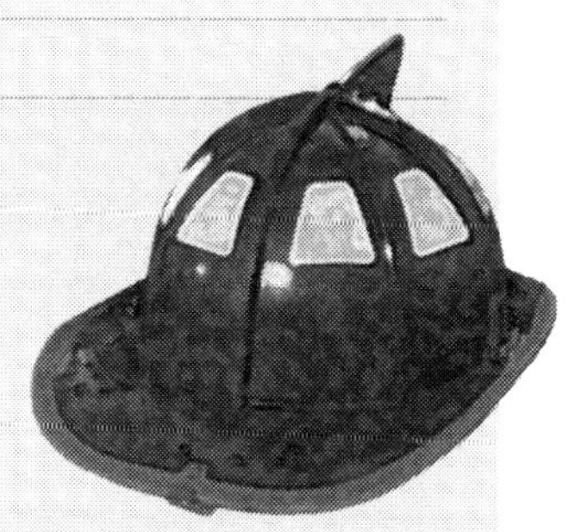

Thoughts & Memories

Name:

Name:

Name:

In a moment, everything can change.

Firefighters know this *better than all.*

Thoughts & Memories

Name:

Name:

Name:

Yet they're willing to serve.

Always on-call.

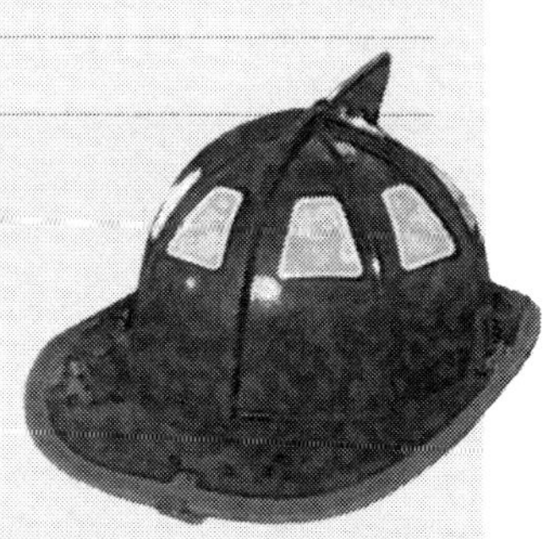

Name:

Name:

Name:

Thoughts & Memories

In a moment, everything can change.

Firefighters know this *better than all.*

Name:

Name:

Name:

Thoughts & Memories

Yet they're willing to serve.

Always on-call.

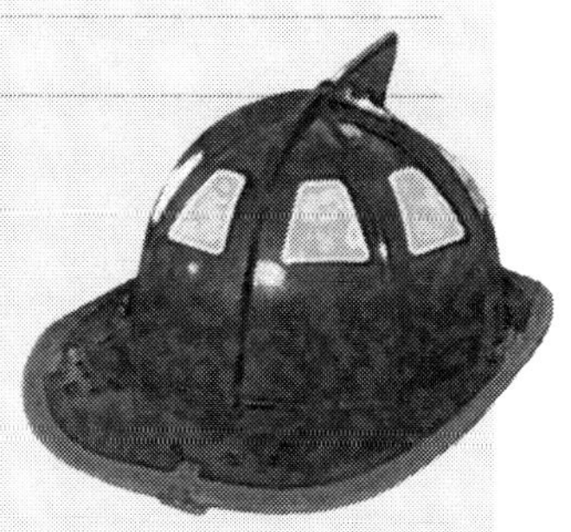

Thoughts & Memories

Name:

Name:

Name:

In a moment, everything can change.

Firefighters know this *better than all.*

Thoughts & Memories

Name: ______________________

Name: ______________________

Name: ______________________

Yet they're willing to serve.

Always on-call.

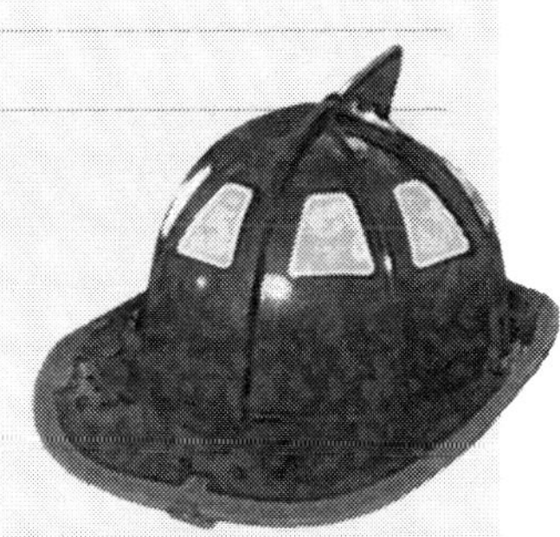

Thoughts & Memories

Name:

Name:

Name:

In a moment, everything can change.

Firefighters know this *better than all.*

Thoughts & Memories

Name:

Name:

Name:

Yet they're willing to serve.

Always on-call.

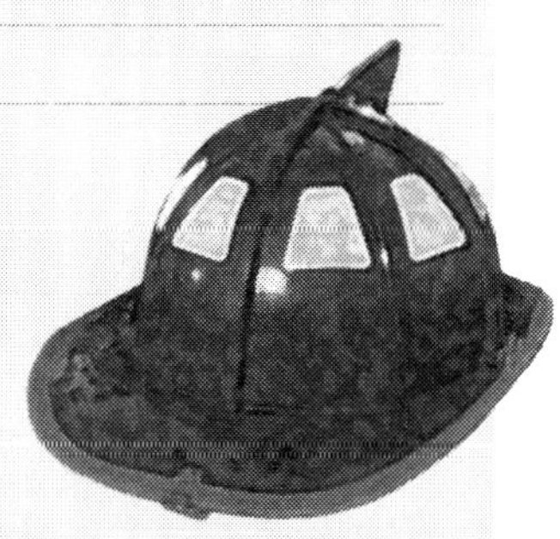

Thoughts & Memories

Name:

Name:

Name:

In a moment, everything can change.

Firefighters know this *better than all.*

Name:

Name:

Name:

Thoughts & Memories

Yet they're willing to serve.

Always on-call.

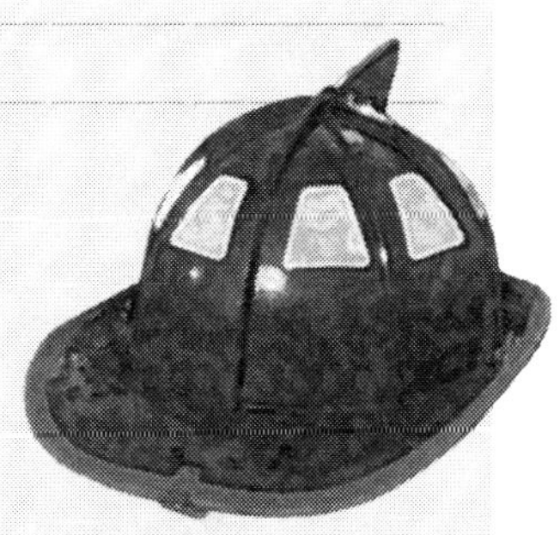

Thoughts & Memories

Name:

Name:

Name:

In a moment, everything can change.

Firefighters know this *better than all.*

Name:

Name:

Name:

Thoughts & Memories

Yet they're willing to serve.

Always on-call.

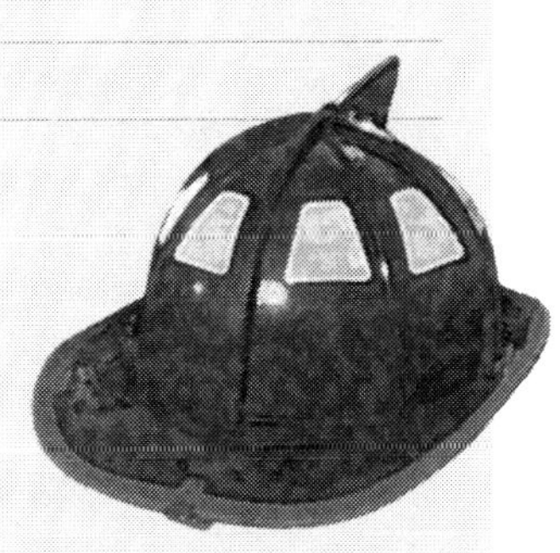

Thoughts & Memories

Name:

Name:

Name:

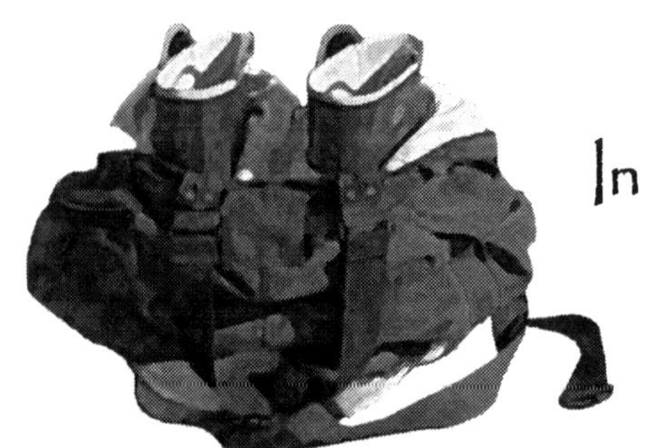

In a moment, everything can change.

Firefighters know this *better than all.*

Name:

Name:

Name:

Thoughts & Memories

Yet they're willing to serve.

Always on-call.

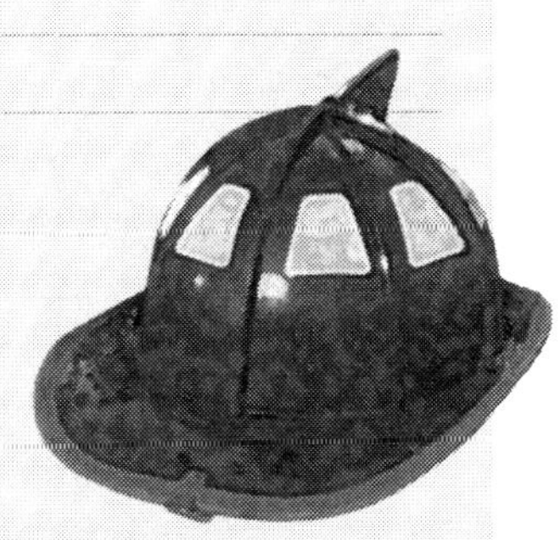

Thoughts & Memories

Name:

Name:

Name:

In a moment, everything can change.

Firefighters know this *better than all.*

Name:

Name:

Name:

Thoughts & Memories

Yet they're willing to serve.

Always on-call.

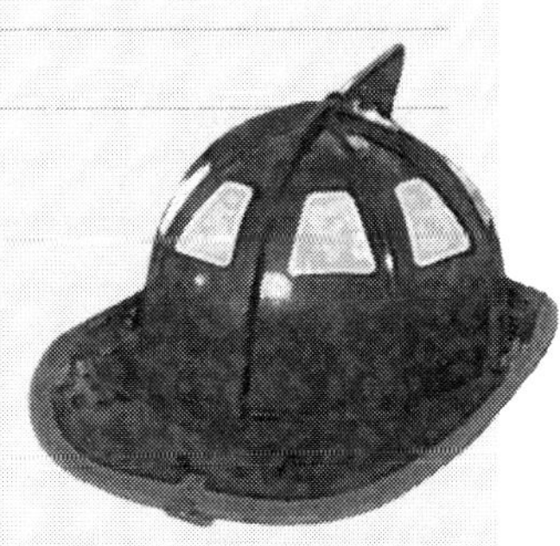

Thoughts & Memories

Name:

Name:

Name:

In a moment, everything can change.

Firefighters know this *better than all.*

Name:

Name:

Name:

Thoughts & Memories

Yet they're willing to serve.

Always on-call.

Thoughts & Memories

Name:

Name:

Name:

In a moment, everything can change.

Firefighters know this *better than all.*

Thoughts & Memories

Name:

Name:

Name:

Yet they're willing to serve.

Always on-call.

Thoughts & Memories

Name:

Name:

Name:

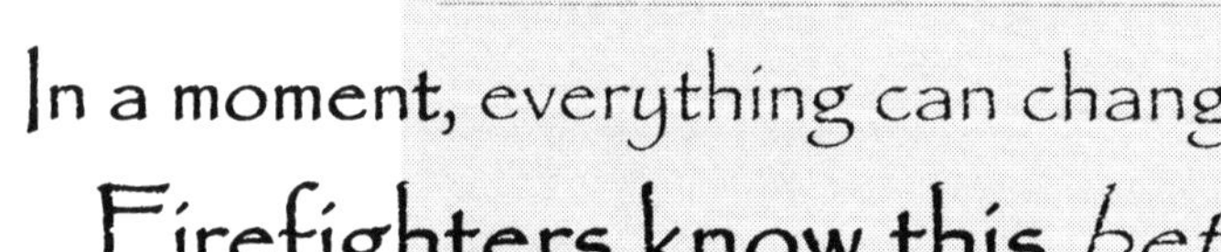

In a moment, everything can change.

Firefighters know this *better than all.*

Name:

Name:

Name:

Thoughts & Memories

Yet they're willing to serve.

Always on-call.

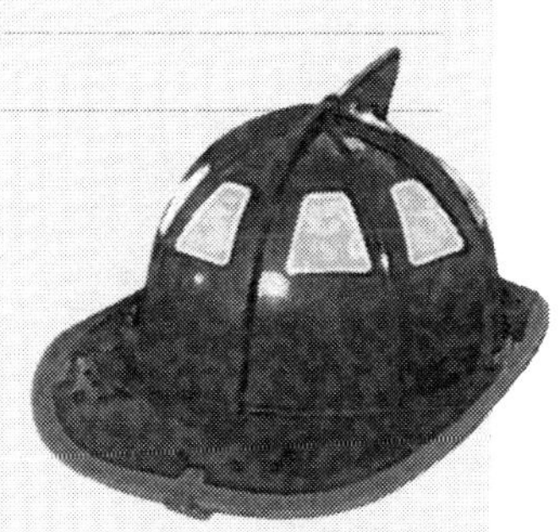

Thoughts & Memories

Name:

Name:

Name:

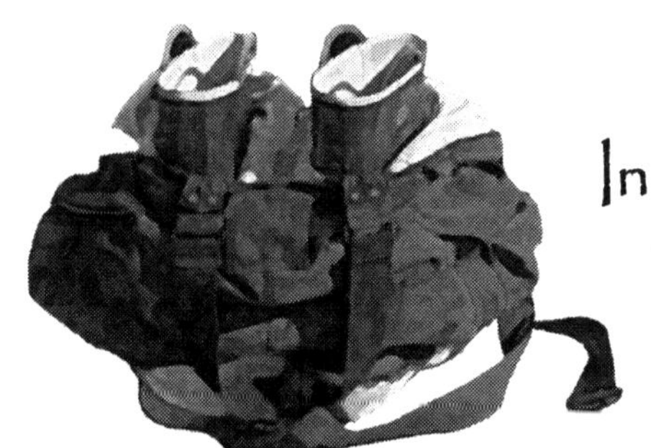

In a moment, everything can change.

Firefighters know this *better than all.*

Name:

Name:

Name:

Thoughts & Memories

Yet they're willing to serve.

Always on-call.

Name:

Name:

Name:

Thoughts & Memories

In a moment, everything can change.

Firefighters know this *better than all.*

Thoughts & Memories

Name:

Name:

Name:

Yet they're willing to serve.

Always on-call.

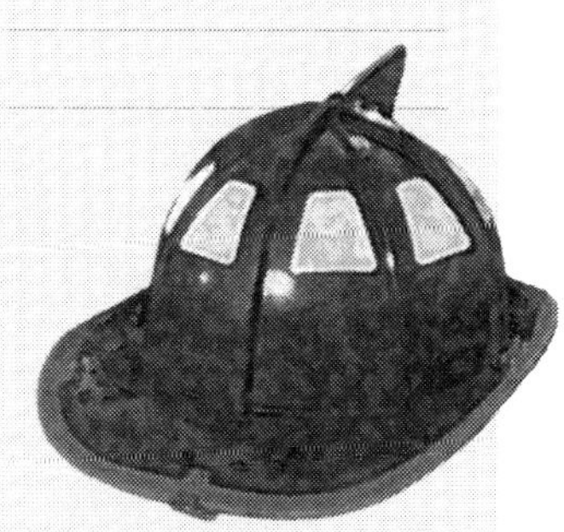

Thoughts & Memories

Name:

Name:

Name:

In a moment, everything can change.

Firefighters know this *better than all.*

Name:

Name:

Name:

Thoughts & Memories

Yet they're willing to serve.

Always on-call.

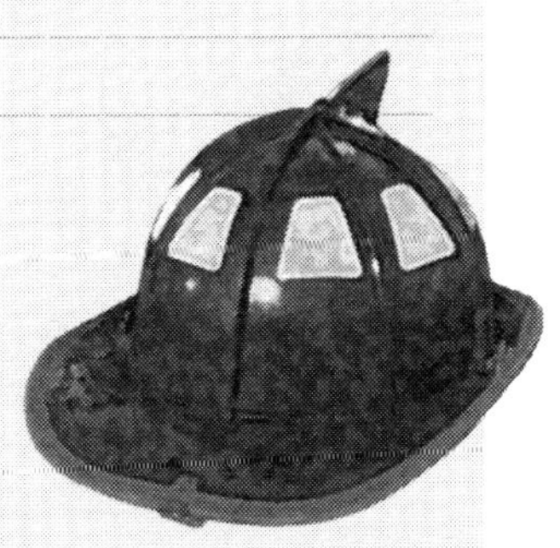

Name:

Name:

Name:

Thoughts & Memories

In a moment, everything can change.

Firefighters know this *better than all.*

Name:

Name:

Name:

Thoughts & Memories

Yet they're willing to serve.

Always on-call.

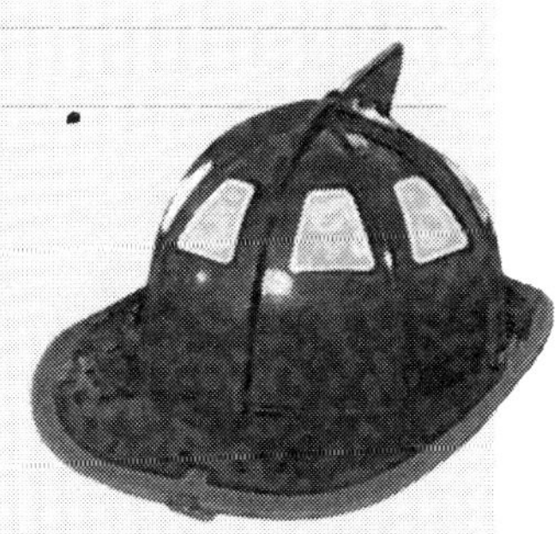

Thoughts & Memories

Name:

Name:

Name:

In a moment, everything can change.

Firefighters know this *better than all.*

Name:

Name:

Name:

Thoughts & Memories

Yet they're willing to serve.

Always on-call.

Thoughts & Memories

Name: ______________________

Name: ______________________

Name: ______________________

In a moment, everything can change.

Firefighters know this *better than all.*

Name:

Name:

Name:

Thoughts & Memories

Yet they're willing to serve.

Always on-call.

Thoughts & Memories

Name:

Name:

Name:

In a moment, everything can change.

Firefighters know this *better than all.*

Name:

Name:

Name:

Thoughts & Memories

Yet they're willing to serve.

Always on-call.

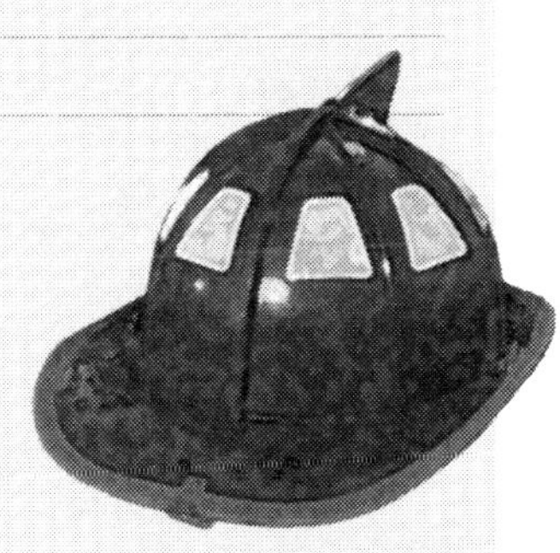

Thoughts & Memories

Name:

Name:

Name:

In a moment, everything can change.

Firefighters know this *better than all.*

Name:

Name:

Name:

Thoughts & Memories

Yet they're willing to serve.

Always on-call.

Thoughts & Memories

Name:

Name:

Name:

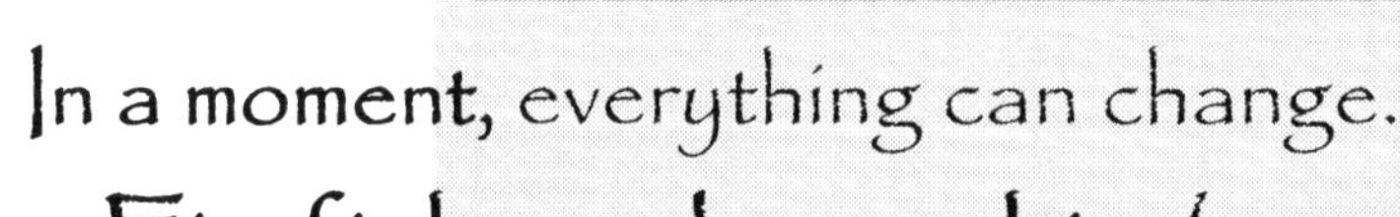

In a moment, everything can change.

Firefighters know this *better than all.*

Thoughts & Memories

Name:

Name:

Name:

Yet they're willing to serve.

Always on-call.

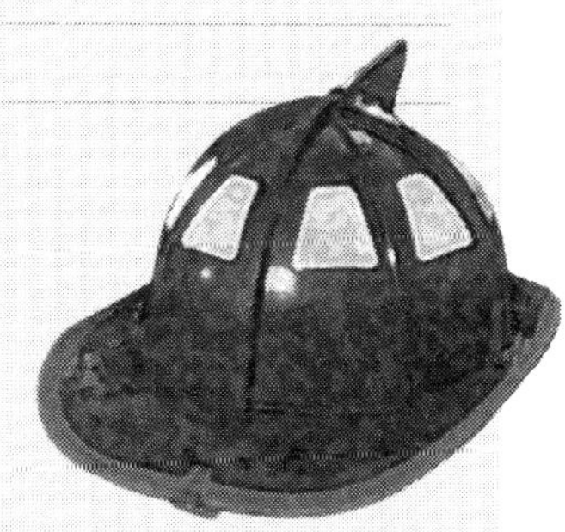

Name:

Name:

Name:

Thoughts & Memories

In a moment, everything can change.

Firefighters know this *better than all.*

Name:

Name:

Name:

Thoughts & Memories

Yet they're willing to serve.

Always on-call.

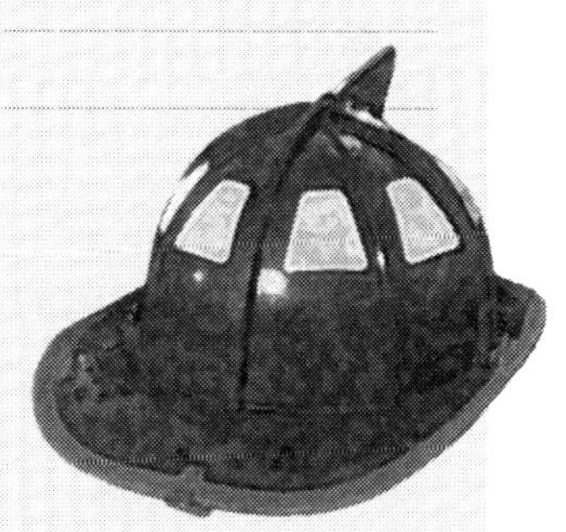

Name:

Name:

Name:

Thoughts & Memories

In a moment, everything can change.

Firefighters know this *better than all.*

Thoughts & Memories

Name:

Name:

Name:

Yet they're willing to serve.

Always on-call.

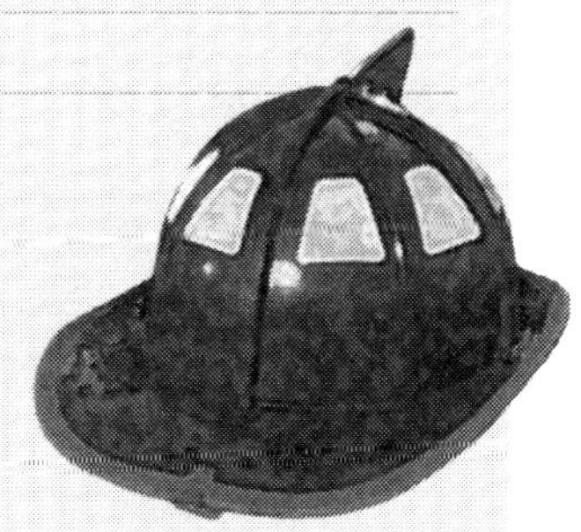

Name:

Name:

Name:

Thoughts & Memories

In a moment, everything can change.

Firefighters know this *better than all.*

Thoughts & Memories

Name:

Name:

Name:

Yet they're willing to serve.

Always on-call.

Thoughts & Memories

Name: ______________________

Name: ______________________

Name: ______________________

In a moment, everything can change.

Firefighters know this *better than all.*

Name:

Name:

Name:

Thoughts & Memories

Yet they're willing to serve.

Always on-call.

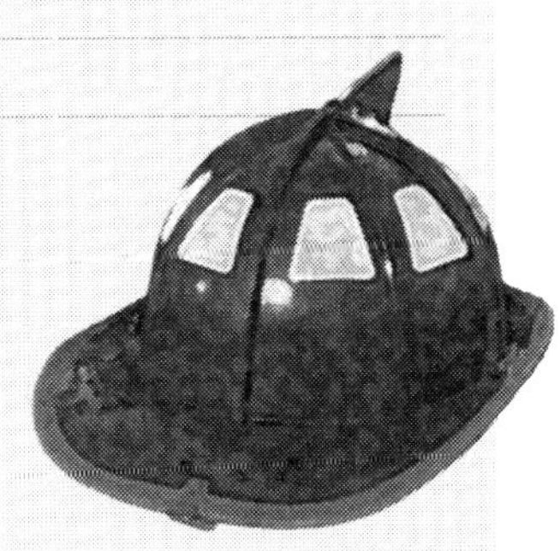

Thoughts & Memories

Name:

Name:

Name:

In a moment, everything can change.

Firefighters know this *better than all.*

Name:

Name:

Name:

Thoughts & Memories

Yet they're willing to serve.

Always on-call.

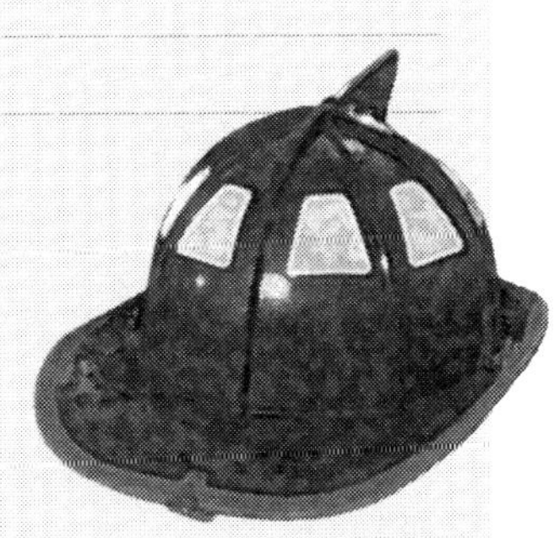

Name:

Name:

Name:

Thoughts & Memories

In a moment, everything can change.

Firefighters know this *better than all.*

Name:

Name:

Name:

Thoughts & Memories

Yet they're willing to serve.

Always on-call.

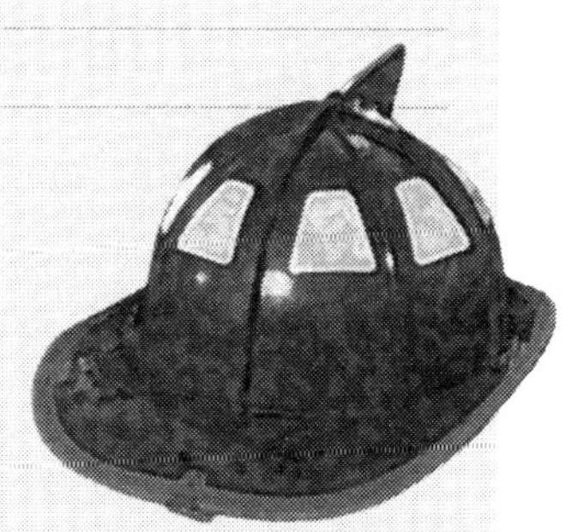

Thoughts & Memories

Name:

Name:

Name:

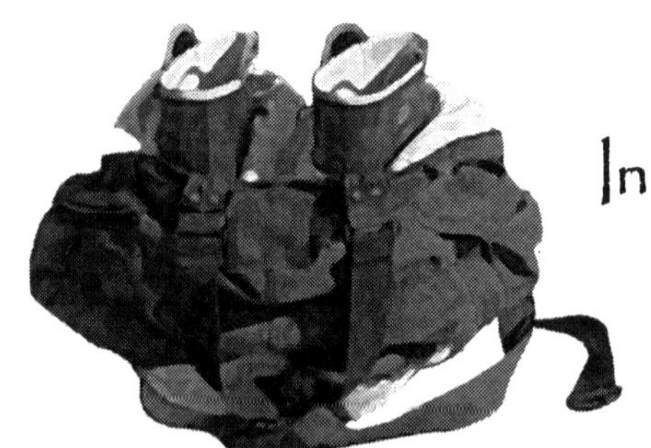

In a moment, everything can change.

Firefighters know this *better than all.*

Thoughts & Memories

Name:

Name:

Name:

Yet they're willing to serve.

Always on-call.

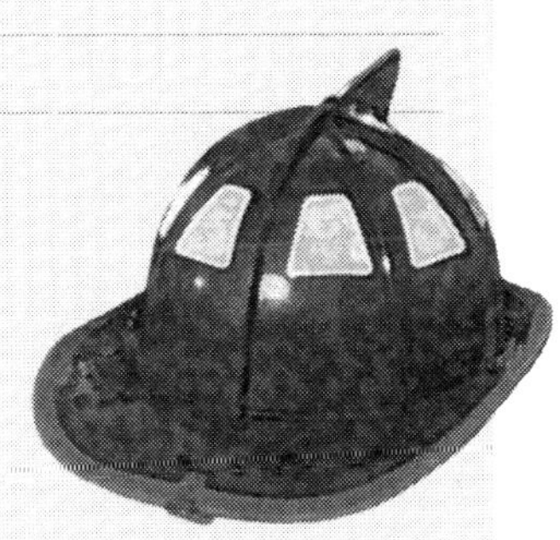

Thoughts & Memories

Name:

Name:

Name:

In a moment, everything can change.

Firefighters know this *better than all.*

Name:

Name:

Name:

Thoughts & Memories

Yet they're willing to serve.

Always on-call.

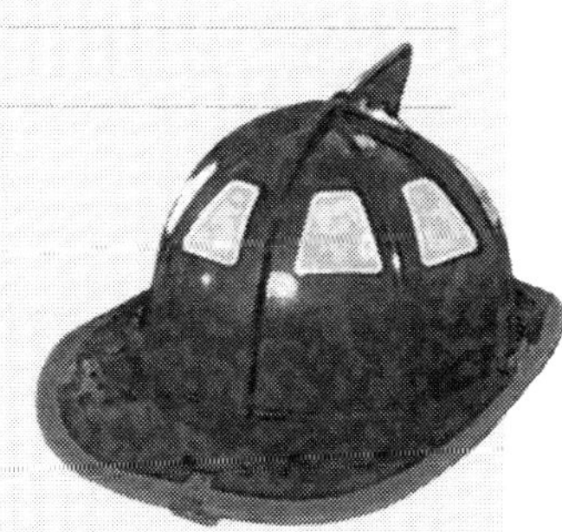

Name:

Name:

Name:

Thoughts & Memories

In a moment, everything can change.

Firefighters know this *better than all.*

Name:

Name:

Name:

Thoughts & Memories

Yet they're willing to serve.

Always on-call.

Name:

Name:

Name:

Thoughts & Memories

ISBN: 978-1-63578-707-8

Current contact information for Libro Studio LLC can be found at www.LibroStudioLLC.com

Made in the USA
Monee, IL
19 February 2025